Collins

SNAP REVISION READING

(for papers 1 and 2)

AQA GCSE 9-1 English Language

AQA GCSE 9-1 ENGLISH LANGUAGE

REVISE TRICKY TOPICS IN A SNAP

Published by Collins
An imprint of HarperCollins*Publishers*
1 London Bridge Street,
London, SE1 9GF

© HarperCollins*Publishers* Limited 2016

9780008218089

First published 2016

14

British Library Cataloguing in Publication Data.

A CIP record of this book is available from the British Library.

Printed in Great Britain by Martins the Printers

ACKNOWLEDGEMENTS

The author and publisher are grateful to the copyright holders for permission to use quoted materials and images.

P.16 Nineteen-Eighty-Four by George Orwell (Copyright © George Orwell, 1949) Reprinted by permission of Bill Hamilton as the Literary Executor of the Estate of the Late Sonia Brownell Orwell.

P.41 'Florence' by Joyce Rackham, from The Times (13 October 1982).

All images are © Shutterstock.com

Every effort has been made to trace copyright holders and obtain their permission for the use of copyright material. The author and publisher will gladly receive information enabling them to rectify any error or omission in subsequent editions. All facts are correct at time of going to press.

How To Use This Book

To get the most out of this revision guide, just work your way through the book in the order it is presented.

This is how it works:

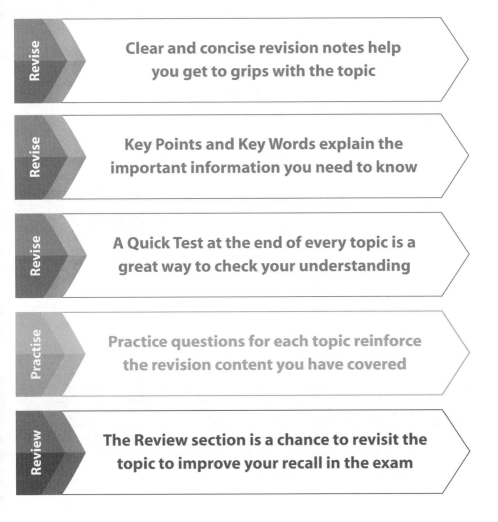

Revise

Clear and concise revision notes help you get to grips with the topic

Revise

Key Points and Key Words explain the important information you need to know

Revise

A Quick Test at the end of every topic is a great way to check your understanding

Practise

Practice questions for each topic reinforce the revision content you have covered

Review

The Review section is a chance to revisit the topic to improve your recall in the exam

Explicit Information and Ideas

You must be able to:

- Identify and interpret explicit information and ideas.

Explicit Information

- **Explicit** information is information that is openly stated. You will find it in the text.
- When answering questions it does not matter whether you think what the writer says is true or plausible. You are required to find the information and repeat it, either in the writer's words or in your own.
- Questions about explicit information normally ask you to list a number of things you can find in the text, for example:
  - List four things the writer tells you about the garden.
  - What do you learn about butterflies from the text?
- Read the text below and list four things the writer tells us about Griselda the cat:

> There were only two places where Griselda would sit in the garden: in the middle of the lawn (to catch the sun) and (if the sun was too hot) in the shade of the plum tree. She sometimes hunted at night and would return in the morning with little presents for us, mice or birds, which she always left in the middle of the kitchen floor to make sure we got them.

- You could say:
  - She would only sit in two places in the garden.
  - She liked to sit in the middle of the lawn.
  - If it was hot she sat under the plum tree.
  - She hunted at night.
  - She brought back mice and birds.
  - She left mice and birds in the kitchen.
    There are six points made here. You can get marks for any four of them but if you put more than four you will not get any extra marks.
- You would not get marks for:
  - She was a cat – you are told this in the question, not in the text.
  - She was friendly – there is no mention of this in the text.
  - There was a plum tree in the garden – true, but it is not about Griselda. It would be a good answer if you were told to 'list four things about the place where Griselda lived'.

Key Point

You may be directed to a section of the text. Make sure you take your information only from that part of the text.

Explicit Ideas

- Explicit ideas are ideas and **opinions** that are openly stated.
- You could be asked, for example:
  - List four ways in which people react to the news.

- List four reasons given for the start of the war.
- Read the text below and **identify** four ideas that, according to the writer, would improve the park:

> Bilberry Recreation Ground is an eyesore. It is time for radical action. Let's start by getting rid of the graffiti – it's not art; it's vandalism. The Victorian benches are also in a sad state – let's restore them. There used to be beautiful flower beds. It's time we planted some new ones. Let's encourage families to return by building a new and exciting playground. What about a kiosk selling cups of tea and ice cream? Finally, may I suggest a change of name? 'Recreation Ground' sounds old-fashioned and dreary. Let's call it Bilberry Park from now on.

- You would get marks for:
  - Get rid of the graffiti.
  - Restore the park benches.
  - Plant new flower beds.
  - Build a playground.
  - Build a refreshment kiosk.
  - Change the name.
- You would not get marks for:
  - It is an eyesore – this is not an idea for improvement.
  - Put a fence round the park – you might think this is a good idea but the writer does not mention it.
  - Take radical action – this is too vague.

Key Point

It does not matter whether you agree with what the writer says. You are being asked to identify the writer's ideas, not yours.

Quick Test

1. What does 'explicit' mean?
2. Can you quote from the text?
3. Can you put the answer in your own words?
4. If you are asked to list four points, do you get an extra mark for giving five?

Key Words

explicit
opinion
identify

Implicit Information and Ideas

You must be able to:

- Identify and interpret implicit information and ideas.

Implicit Information

- Implicit information is not stated openly. It is **implied**, so you have to 'read between the lines' to **infer** it from the text.
- Sometimes information is implied by saying what is not true:
  - He was not a happy child.
  This implies that he was sad.
- One piece of information can be implied by giving another:
  - They painted their garden shed blue.
  We can infer from this that they had a garden. Otherwise it would not be a 'garden' shed.

> ### Key Point
>
> To imply something means to suggest something without expressly stating it. If you infer something you understand something which has been implied.

Implicit Ideas

- Similarly, writers can make their views and feelings clear without openly stating them:
  - I would rather stick pins in my eyes than sit through another maths lesson.
  This implies that the writer does not like maths.
- When you infer meaning and explain what you have inferred, you are **interpreting** implicit information or ideas.
- Sometimes we infer a writer's views or feelings by putting together a number of pieces of **evidence**. Read the following text:

One thing that really annoys me is the way they constantly scratch themselves. And every dog I've ever met has had smelly breath. As for the constant barking and yapping! Give me a nice quiet cat or hamster any day.

If you were asked whether the writer likes dogs, you could only answer 'no'. He or she does not ever say 'I don't like dogs', but gives three negative opinions about them and no positive ones.

True or False?

- You might get a question in the form of a tick box exercise, for example: 'Choose four statements below that are TRUE'.
- Read the following passage:

I Left My Heart on Bilberry Rec

by Mary Goodenough

Bilberry Rec is a part of my past. It didn't have wonderful facilities or beautiful vistas. There were no rose gardens or tea shops, no adventure playgrounds and certainly no 'wild meadows'. There were a few trees and hedges, the 'swing park' and a football pitch.

It was what it said it was: a recreation ground, a place where people of all ages went for recreation. Small children played on the swings and didn't often bash their heads on the concrete floor. Bigger children played football or cricket – or just fought. Courting couples walked hand in hand along the muddy paths or snogged on the broken benches. Pensioners walked their dogs and everyone used it as a short cut.

I know times have changed. And my head tells me the new Bilberry Park will be much nicer (and cleaner and safer) than the old Rec, but my heart wants it left just as it is. It's a sure sign of getting older – an attack of illogical nostalgia.

- Which of the following statements are true?
    1. Mary Goodenough has happy memories of Bilberry Rec.
    2. There was a rose garden in Bilberry Rec.
    3. The new park will have better facilities than the old Rec.
    4. Goodenough didn't feel safe in the Rec.
    5. Bilberry Rec was a beautiful place.
    6. Sometimes there were accidents in the swing park.
    7. Goodenough understands why things should change.
    8. Bilberry Rec is going to be built on.
- Numbers 1, 3, 6 and 7 are true.
    - 1 is implied by references to her 'heart' and nostalgia.
    - 3 is implied by referring to what the old Rec didn't have and calling the new park 'nicer...cleaner and safer'.
    - 6 is implied by saying that it didn't happen 'often'.
    - 7 is implied by saying that her 'head' tells her it will be better and that her nostalgia is 'illogical'.

> **Key Point**
>
> When completing a 'true or false' exercise, make sure you fill in the correct number of boxes.

> **Quick Test**
>
> 1. Who implies, the writer or the reader?
> 2. Who infers?
> 3. Should you give your opinion?
> 4. What happens if you tick/shade too many boxes?

> **Key Words**
>
> implicit
> imply
> infer
> interpret
> evidence

Synthesis and Summary

You must be able to:

- Select and synthesize evidence from different texts
- Summarize the content of texts.

Synthesis

- **Synthesis** is the bringing together of parts to make a whole. In exams this usually takes the form of writing about two different texts.
- In Paper 2 of the English Language exam you will have to compare the **content** of two non-fiction texts.
- The texts will be about similar subjects but one will have been written in the nineteenth and one in the twenty-first century, so it is likely that there will be differences in attitudes as well as in the things and people described.

Summary

- A **summary** is a shortened version of something, keeping the main points but leaving out unnecessary detail.
- When you write a summary do not add your own thoughts or comment on the writers' style or techniques.
- You should use evidence from the text in the form of short quotations but most of the answer should be in your own words. Do not copy out huge chunks of the text.
- Remember you are being asked to summarize two texts, so write about them both at equal length.
  - Do not write about one and then the other.
  - Write about both throughout your answer, summarising different aspects of the texts as you go.

Approaching the Question

- Read the question carefully. It will not just ask you to summarize the texts; it will have a particular focus, for example:
  - Write a summary of the differences between Mary and Jordan.
  - Summarize the different feelings of the writers about school.
- **Skim read** both texts.
- Underline or highlight the main points in the texts.
- You might want to do a (very quick) plan, listing **differences** (and **similarities** if asked for).
- Focus on the question.
- Don't repeat yourself.
- Don't waste time on an introductory and concluding paragraph.
- Write in proper sentences and paragraphs, using connectives.

> **Key Point**
>
> Remember to look for both explicit and implicit information and ideas.

Example

- Below are two short extracts from texts about sea voyages. Think about what you would include if you were asked to write a summary of the differences between the voyages:

Daily Southern Cross, 21 October 1859

The *Mermaid* [...] arrived in harbour on Wednesday at 4 a.m. She left Liverpool on 11th July at 5 p.m. Passengers have been very healthy during the voyage; three infants died, and one birth occurred. The passengers speak highly of Captain White and officers.

Southern Star, 19 July 2014

After three weeks the luxury liner *Ariadne* finally arrived home and the passengers disembarked from the journey one of them described as 'a floating nightmare'. For the last week almost a quarter of the passengers had been confined to their cabins with mild food poisoning and many are now demanding their money back.

- You could pick out the following differences:

Mermaid	Ariadne
Journey over three months	Three-week journey
Passengers 'healthy' – three infants died	Food poisoning
Passengers praise captain and crew	Passengers demand money back

- A paragraph summarizing the differences might read:

> The **Mermaid's** journey lasted over three months; **Ariadne's** took three weeks. The **Mermaid's** passengers are 'healthy' but the **Ariadne's** have food poisoning. However, 'three infants died' on the **Mermaid**, suggesting that not everyone was healthy. Nevertheless, it would seem that the Victorian passengers were happier than the modern ones, as they 'speak highly' of the crew rather than complaining.

Quick Test

1. Should the summary be shorter than the original text?
2. Should you use quotations in your summary?
3. Can you write about just one of the texts?
4. Should you discuss the writers' use of language in your answer?

Key Words

synthesis
content
summary
skim read
difference
similarity

Referring to the Text

You must be able to:

- Select appropriate and relevant examples from texts
- Use textual references to support and illustrate your interpretation of the texts.

Referring to the Text

- You can **refer** to a text by **paraphrasing** the text or by **quoting** from the text.
- For all Language questions and some Literature questions, you will have a text in front of you from which you can take your examples.
- For other Literature questions you will have to rely on your memory, so it is a good idea to learn some significant quotations.

Paraphrasing

- Paraphrasing means putting something into your own words. It is useful for summing up, for example:

> The writer gives us a number of examples of cruelty to animals such as neglect and physical violence, which he describes in very vivid terms.

- When you are writing about a longer text, such as a novel, you might not need to quote because you are writing about events or feelings and the exact wording is not important:

> Lydia clearly does not think much about her family's reputation. When she returns from London she does not express any shame at her behaviour but boasts about being married.

Key Point

It is very important to refer to the text in your answers, both in English Language and English Literature exams.

Using Quotations

- A **quotation** is a word or phrase taken directly from the text. Indicate that you are quoting by putting inverted commas (or quotation marks) around the quotation.
- There are three main ways to set out your quotations.
- If your quotation consists of just a few words (or even one word) and fits naturally into your sentence, you simply put it into inverted commas (quotation marks):

> At the start of the soliloquy Juliet refers to 'love-performing night' but later it becomes a 'sober suited matron all in black'.

This is called **embedding**. Examiners like you to embed and it should be the method you use most often.

- If the quotation will not fit easily into your sentence but is fairly short (no more than 40 words of prose or one line of verse), put a colon (:) before it, continue on the same line and use inverted commas:

> Benvolio passionately asserts that he is not lying: 'This is the truth or let Benvolio die.'

- If you want to use a longer quotation, leave a line and indent. You must indent the whole quotation. When quoting verse, end the lines where they end in the original. Do not use inverted commas:

> This opposition will inevitably cause problems for the lovers and Juliet expresses her dilemma:
>
> > My only love sprung from my only hate!
> > Too early seen unknown and known too late!
>
> The use of paradox emphasizes her confusion.

Using PEE

- Remember to use PEE (Point, Evidence, Explanation).
- First make your **point**, saying what you want to say about the text.
- Then give your **evidence**, either in the form of a paraphrase or a quotation.
- Finally, **explain** or explore the evidence you have given.

> The writer is very concerned about what he sees as widespread cruelty to domestic animals. He mentions the 'heartless neglect' of some dogs by their owners. The use of this emotive adjective paints the owners as villains and appeals to the compassion of the readers.

Here the first sentence makes the point, the second gives the evidence in quotation marks, and the third explains/explores the evidence.

Analysing Language 1

You must be able to:

- Explain, comment on and analyse how writers use language
- Use relevant subject terminology to support your views.

Diction and Register

- **Diction** and **register** both refer to the writer's choice of words or vocabulary.
- Most texts you read will be in Standard English. Sometimes, however, you will come across a text that uses a lot of non-standard words, for example slang and dialect words.
- Their use can tell you something about the writer, the narrator, certain characters or the audience at whom the text is aimed.
- Writers might use specialized diction: for example, a lot of scientific or medical terms. The use of such language shows that the text is aimed at people who are interested in the subject and probably already know quite a lot about it.
- Writers might use words and expressions associated with a particular subject – for example, war or nature – for rhetorical or figurative purposes. Sometimes their word choice is referred to as a **semantic field**. We can often infer their attitude to the subject from their choice of semantic field.

Parts of Speech (Word Classes)

- **Nouns** are naming words.
  - **Concrete nouns** name objects (chair, mountain).
  - **Abstract nouns** name ideas and feelings (love, suspicion).
  - **Proper nouns** have capital letters and name individual people (Jelena), places (Warsaw), days of the week (Saturday), months (April) etc.
  - A 'noun phrase' is a group of words built around a noun.
- **Adjectives** describe nouns (the **red** house; his **undying** love).
- **Verbs** are doing, feeling and being words. You might comment on whether verbs are:
  - in the past tense (she walked; he was thinking)
  - in the present tense (she is walking; he thinks)
  - or in the future tense (we are going to walk; you will go).
- **Adverbs** describe verbs, telling us how something is being done, for example, she spoke **slowly**; he writes **carefully**.
- **Pronouns** stand in for other words, usually nouns. Whether the writer uses first person (I/we), second person (you) or third person (he/she/they) can make a difference to how we read the text. 'I' makes the text more personal to the writer. 'We' and 'you' aim to involve the reader more in the text. There are different types of pronouns.

> **Key Point**
>
> When we talk about 'parts of speech' or 'word class' we are referring to what words do in sentences. It is important that you can identify these so that you can refer easily to them in a way that shows you understand their function: for example, 'The writer uses a lot of adjectives associated with war to describe the scene.'

Personal pronouns	Relative pronouns
I/me	who
we/us	whom
you	whose
he/him	that
she/her	which
it	
they/them	

- **Prepositions** are used to express the relationship between nouns (or noun phrases) and other parts of the sentence or clause:
  - We went **to** the cinema.
  - The cat is **under** the table.
- **Conjunctions** join words, phrases and clauses: for example, 'and', 'but', 'although', 'because'. A conjunction is a type of connective but the two words are not interchangeable. Other types of word and phrase, including relative pronouns and adverbs, can also act as connectives
- **Determiners** come before nouns and help to define them. The most common are the definite article (the) and the indefinite article (a/an). Other examples of determiners are 'this', 'both' and 'some'.

Key Point

If you are not confident about identifying parts of speech it is better to avoid mentioning them. Using incorrect terminology will not impress the examiner.

Key Words

diction
register
vocabulary
semantic field
noun
concrete noun
abstract noun
proper noun
adjective
verb
adverb
pronoun
preposition
conjunction
determiner

Quick Test

Read this sentence:
The old horse was munching thoughtfully on his oats.
Identify:
1. Two nouns
2. A verb
3. An adjective
4. A preposition
5. An adverb

Analysing Language 2

You must be able to:

- Explain, comment on and analyse how writers use language
- Use relevant subject terminology to support your views.

Connotation

- A connotation is an implied meaning. Words can have associations other than their literal meanings. For example, red indicates danger or anger. 'Heart' has connotations of love and sincerity.

> **Key Point**
>
> Writers use language to affect and influence their readers.

Emotive Language

- Writers often seek to arouse certain feelings or emotions in the reader, for example, pity or anger. This can be done by using **emotive language**: words and phrases that have certain connotations.
- A reporter writing about a crime could write:

  Burglars stole some jewellery from Mr Bolton's house.

  This just tells us the facts. A writer who wanted to influence our emotions might write:

  Heartless burglars stole jewellery of great sentimental value from frail pensioner Albert Bolton. ◄───

The adjective 'heartless' makes the burglars sound deliberately cruel, and 'frail' emphasizes the weakness of the victim, while the phrase 'of great sentimental value' tells us how important the jewellery was to Mr Bolton. This increases our sympathy for him.

Rhetorical Language

- **Rhetoric** is the art of speaking. Effective speakers have developed ways of influencing their audiences. Writers also use rhetorical techniques to affect readers.
- **Hyperbole** is another word for exaggeration:

  Councillor Williams is the most obnoxious man ever to disgrace this council chamber.

- Lists of three are used to hammer home a point:

  Friends, Romans, countrymen.

- **Repetition** is used to emphasize the importance of the point being made:

  Victory at all costs, victory in spite of all terror, victory however long and hard the road may be; for without victory there is no survival.

- **Rhetorical questions** are questions which do not need an answer. Sometimes the writer gives an answer:

  Can we do this? Yes, we can.

  Sometimes they are left unanswered to make the reader think about the answer:

  What kind of people do they think we are?

Sound

- The sound of words can make a difference to their meaning and effect.
- Onomatopoeia is the use of words which sound like their meaning:

  The door creaked open and clunked shut.

- Alliteration, the use of a series of words starting with the same sound, is common in newspaper headlines as well as in poetry and other literary texts:
  - Brave Bella battles burglars.
  - Storm'd at with shot and shell.
- When you see alliteration, think about why the writer uses a particular sound. Some consonants ('d', 'k', 'g') are hard. Others ('s', 'f') are soft. 'P' and 'b' have an explosive quality.
- The repetition of 's' sounds is also referred to as sibilance.
- Assonance is the use of a series of similar vowel sounds for effect:

  From the bronzey soft sky…Tipples over and spills down.

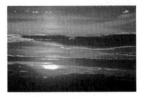

Imagery

- Literal imagery is the use of description to convey a mood or atmosphere. A description of a storm might create an atmosphere of violence and danger.
- Figurative imagery uses an image of one thing to tell us about another.
  - Similes compare one thing to another directly, using 'like' or 'as':

    Straight and slight as a young larch tree.

  - Metaphors imply a comparison. Something is written about *as if it were* something else:

    Beth was a real angel.

  - Personification makes a thing, idea or feeling into a person:

    At my back I always hear
    Time's winged chariot hurrying near.

  - The personification of nature, giving it human qualities, is also called pathetic fallacy:

    The clouds wept with joy.

    This term can also be applied to a literal description in which nature or the weather reflects the feelings of characters.
  - A symbol is an object which represents a feeling or idea, for example a dove to represent peace.

> **Key Point**
>
> Imagery is usually associated with literary texts, such as poems. However, non-fiction texts also use imagery to paint pictures in the readers' minds.

> **Key Words**
>
> connotation
> emotive language
> rhetoric
> hyperbole
> repetition
> rhetorical question
> onomatopoeia
> alliteration
> sibilance
> assonance
> imagery
> simile
> metaphor
> personification
> pathetic fallacy
> symbol

> ## Quick Test
>
> Of which literary techniques are the following examples?
> 1. Macbeth doth murder sleep.
> 2. Ill met by moonlight.
> 3. I wandered lonely as a cloud.
> 4. You were sunrise to me.

Analysing Form and Structure

You must be able to:

- Explain, comment on and analyse how writers use form and structure
- Use relevant subject terminology to support your views.

Form and Structure

- The structure of a text is the way in which it is organized: for example, the order in which information is given or events described.
- The terms 'structure' and 'form' are both used to describe how a text is set out on the page.

Openings

- The beginning (opening) of a text is very important as it has to draw in the readers and encourage them to continue reading.
- Some texts begin by giving an overview of the subject, indicating what the text is going to be about:

> There are thousands of varieties of butterfly. In this article I will discuss some of the most common.

- A writer might explain why he or she has decided to write:

> Lewis's views about youth unemployment are fundamentally wrong.

- Fiction writers can use their openings to introduce characters or settings:

> 'I shall never forget Tony's face,' said the carrier.

- Texts can also start with dramatic statements, designed to shock, surprise or intrigue:

> It was a bright cold day in April, and the clocks were striking thirteen.

Endings

- Fiction writers might give a neat conclusion: for example, with the solving of a crime or a marriage:

> Reader, I married him.

- They might prefer to leave us with a sense of mystery or suspense:

> 'Who are they?' asked George [...]
> '*Wolves*.'

- Writers of essays and articles usually end by drawing together their main points and reaching a conclusion.
- Some texts end with a question or even an instruction:

> Get out there now and use your vote!

> ### Key Point
>
> You should consider why the writer has decided to arrange things in a particular way and the effect of this on the reader.

Chronological Order

- **Chronological order** gives events in the order in which they happened. This is the most common way of ordering fiction, and non-fiction texts such as histories, biographies and travel writing.
- Writers might, however, start at the end of the story or somewhere in the middle before going back to recap previous events in 'flashbacks'.
- **Reverse chronological order** means starting with the latest event and working backwards. You will see this in **blogs** and discussion forums.

Other Ways of Ordering Texts

- Some texts start with general information and move on to more detailed information and explanation.
- A text giving a point of view might build up to what the writer thinks are the most persuasive arguments.
- Information can be arranged in **alphabetical order**, as in dictionaries and encyclopaedias.
- Texts sometimes rank things or people in order of importance or popularity, as in a music chart, either starting with the best and working down or starting with the worst and working up.

Divisions

- Books are usually divided into **chapters**, sometimes with titles or numbers.
- Most prose is arranged in **paragraphs**, while verse is often divided into **stanzas**. Make sure you use the correct terminology.
- Other devices used to divide up text include **bullet points**, numbering and **text boxes**. Headlines and subheadings help to guide readers through the text.

Analysing Structure

- When analysing a short text, or an extract from a longer text, think about how and why the writer changes focus from one paragraph or section to another, perhaps moving from a general description to something more detailed, from a group of people to a particular character, or from description to action or speech.

> **Key Point**
>
> Texts, especially longer texts, are often divided into sections. These give order to their contents and help readers find their way through the text.

> **Key Words**
>
> opening
> conclusion
> chronological order
> reverse chronological order
> blog
> alphabetical order
> chapter
> paragraph
> stanza
> bullet point
> text box

> **Quick Test**
>
> Put the following in:
> 1. chronological order
> 2. reverse chronological order
> 3. alphabetical order
>   a) December 2014
>   b) January 2002
>   c) April 2011
>   d) November 2011

1 Read the passage below. List four reactions that people have to Scrooge. [4]

From *A Christmas Carol* by Charles Dickens

Nobody ever stopped him in the street to say, with gladsome looks, 'My dear Scrooge, how are you? When will you come to see me?' No beggars implored him to bestow a trifle;[1] no children asked him what it was o'clock; no man or woman ever once in all his life inquired the way to such and such a place, of Scrooge. Even the blindmen's dogs appeared to know him; and when they saw him coming on, would tug their owners into doorways and up courts; and then would wag their tails as though they said, 'No eye at all is better than an evil eye, dark master!'

[1] *bestow a trifle* – to give a small amount

_____

_____

_____

_____

2 How does Dickens use language to give us an impression of Scrooge's character? You could comment on his use of:
- words and phrases
- language feature and techniques
- sentence forms.

Write your answer on a separate piece of paper. [8]

3 Read the passage below.

From a letter written by Charles Lamb to William Wordsworth

London, January 30, 1801

I ought before this to have replied to your very kind invitation into Cumberland. With you and your sister I could gang[1] anywhere. But I am afraid whether I shall ever be able to afford so desperate a Journey. Separate from the pleasure of your company, I don't much care if I never see a mountain in my life. I have passed all my days in London [...] The lighted shops of the Strand and Fleet Street, the innumerable trades, tradesmen and customers, coaches, waggons, playhouses, all the bustle and wickedness round about Covent Garden, the very women of the Town, the Watchmen, drunken scenes, rattles;[2]—life awake, if you awake, at all hours of the night, the impossibility of being dull in Fleet Street, the crowds, the very dirt & mud, the Sun shining upon houses and pavements, the print shops, the old *Book* stalls, [...] coffee houses, steams of soup from kitchens, the pantomimes, London itself a pantomime and a masquerade, all these things work themselves into my mind and feed me without a power of satiating me. The wonder of these sights impels me into night walks about the crowded streets, and I often shed tears in the motley Strand from fullness of joy at so much *Life*.—All these emotions must be strange to you. So are your rural emotions to me [...]

My attachments are all local, purely local.—I have no passion [...] to groves and valleys.—The rooms where I was born, the furniture which has been before my eyes all my life, a book case which has followed me about (like a faithful dog, only exceeding him in knowledge) wherever I have moved, old tables, streets, squares, where I have sunned myself, my old school,—these are my mistresses. Have I not enough, without your mountains?

[1] *gang* – a dialect word for 'go'
[2] *rattles* – constant chatterers

Which of the following statements are TRUE? Tick the correct boxes.

a) Charles Lamb hates London. ☐

b) He has always lived in London. ☐

c) He finds life in the city exciting. ☐

d) He does not like going out after dark. ☐

e) He thinks Wordsworth will find it strange that he does not like the countryside. ☐

f) He likes to spend time with Wordsworth and his sister. ☐

g) He loves climbing mountains. ☐

h) He is thinking of buying some new furniture. ☐ [4]

4 Now read this article and write a summary of the differences between Weston's and Lamb's attitudes to city life. [8]

I'm a City-Hater – Get Me out of Here!

by Malcolm Weston

I've had enough. I'm leaving. Who was it who said that when a man is tired of London he's tired of life? Well, I don't think I'm tired of life – I'd like to go on living as long as I can – but I'm fed up to the back teeth with London. It's dirty. It's noisy. You can barely move in Oxford Street sometimes. Everything's expensive (how can anyone afford to live here?). And everyone is so bad-tempered. I know it's meant to be terribly lively and exciting but, frankly, I'm bored with it. Sorry, Londoners. It's nothing personal: I don't really like any cities – or towns. So I'm off home. And this time next week you'll find me (if you can – it's a bit off the beaten track) halfway up a mountain somewhere in the Lake District, looking up at the sky and listening to the sound of silence.

5 Read the passage below (Source A), in which Charlotte Brontë describes how she and her sisters, Anne and Emily, went about publishing their poems.

From Charlotte Brontë's *Biographical Notice of Ellis and Acton Bell*

We agreed to arrange a small selection of our poems, and, if possible, get them printed. Averse to personal publicity, we veiled our own names under those of Currer, Ellis, and Acton Bell; the ambiguous choice being dictated by a sort of conscientious scruple at assuming Christian names positively masculine, while we did not like to declare ourselves women, because – without at that time suspecting that our mode of writing and thinking was not what is called 'feminine' – we had a vague impression that authoresses are liable to be looked on with prejudice [...]

The bringing out of our little book was hard work. As was to be expected, neither we nor our poems were at all wanted; but for this we had been prepared at the outset; though inexperienced ourselves, we had read the experience of others. The great puzzle lay in the difficulty of getting answers of any kind from the publishers to whom we applied. Being greatly harassed by this obstacle I ventured to apply to the Messrs. Chambers, of Edinburgh, for a word of advice; they may have forgotten the circumstance, but I have not, for from them I received a brief and business-like, but civil and sensible reply, on which we acted, and at last made a way.

The book was printed; it is scarcely known, and all of it that merits to be known are the poems of Ellis Bell. The fixed conviction I held, and hold of the worth of these poems has not indeed received the confirmation of much favourable criticism; but I must retain it notwithstanding.

Which of the following statements are TRUE? Tick the correct boxes.

a) All three sisters contributed poems to the book. ☐

b) They wrote under their own names. ☐

c) They felt that critics were prejudiced against female authors. ☐

d) They were not keen on publicity. ☐

e) They had lots of replies from publishers. ☐

f) Charlotte Brontë found the advice of Chambers sensible and useful. ☐

g) The book was a great success. ☐

h) Emily's (Ellis's) poems were the worst thing about the book. ☐

i) Bringing out the book was simple, easy work. ☐

j) The sisters were all very experienced at working with publishers. ☐   [4]

6 Now read this article (Source B) and write a summary of the differences between Brontë's and Fordyce's experience.

How I Made My Own Luck

by Lily Fordyce

People often ask me for advice about writing, which really means they want me to give them the magic key that opens the door to publication, fame and fortune. I can't promise any of that. All I can do is say how it was for me, and that what worked for me won't work for everyone. There are two essential ingredients: hard work and luck. Some people say you make your own luck. If that's true, this is the luck I made:

1. I started reading out my poetry in public. It wasn't that hard for me. I'm one of life's show-offs. I was welcomed with enthusiasm, especially because I'm a woman. 'We don't get enough women' was a cry I heard again and again.

2. I sent my poems to every poetry magazine going, whether they pay or not (mostly they don't) and very soon I was seeing my work in print.

3. I entered almost every competition I could find.

And finally, I won a competition, which led to my first book, which did very well – and here I am: a hardworking and very lucky poet.

_____

_____

_____

_____

_____

_____

_____

_____

_____ [8]

7 Look again at Source B. How does Fordyce use language to convey her feelings about becoming a poet? You could include her choice of:

- words and phrases
- language features and techniques
- sentence forms.

Write your answer on a separate piece of paper. [12]

Creative Reading 1

You must be able to:

- Read and understand a range of literature
- Critically evaluate literature texts.

Story Structure

- Most novels and stories begin by 'setting the scene', introducing characters or places and giving us a sense of the world we are entering.
- That world might be very like our own world but it could be unfamiliar, perhaps because the story is set in a different country or a different time.
- The writer might even, like Tolkien, have invented a complete fantasy world.
- This part of a story is called exposition and can take a chapter or more, or maybe just a few lines.
- The event that really gets the story going is sometimes called the inciting incident. This can be dramatic and shocking, like Pip's encounter with the convict at the beginning of *Great Expectations*, or it can be a seemingly ordinary event, like Darcy coming to stay with Bingley in *Pride and Prejudice*.
- Inciting incidents change the lives of the protagonists (the main characters) for ever.

> ### Key Point
>
> Every story has a beginning, a middle and an end. The extracts you will be given might come from any part of the story.

- During the course of a story there are usually several **turning points**. Turning points are events which change the direction of the story for good or ill. Sometimes we can see them coming; sometimes they are unexpected and surprising 'twists' in the plot.
- Towards the end, most stories reach a **climax**, or denouement, when things come to a conclusion, sometimes happily as in a fairy tale, sometimes not. This is the event the whole story has been building up to.
- The climax is not always at the end of the story. Most writers take some time to reflect on how things have turned out.
- Endings quite often refer back to openings, giving a sense of how things have changed.

Narrative Perspectives

- Many stories are told in the first person singular ('I'), so that we see the story through the eyes of one of the characters, usually the **protagonist**, for example, Jane in *Jane Eyre* or Harri in *Pigeon English*. This encourages us to empathize with them.
- Sometimes the **narrator** is another character, acting more as an observer and putting some distance between the reader and the protagonist. Dr Watson in the Sherlock Holmes stories is an example of this.
- Each narrator has his or her own 'voice'. In *Pigeon English*, for example, the kind of language the narrator uses tells us about his background and culture.
- A writer might use several different narrators so that we get different characters' experiences and points of view: Mary Shelley does this in *Frankenstein*.
- In a 'third-person **narrative**' the narrator is not involved in the story at all. If there is a sense of the narrator's 'voice', it is the voice of the author. This gives the writer the opportunity of sharing with us the thoughts, feelings and experiences of many characters.
- A narrator who can see everything in this way is called an **omniscient narrator**.
- Sometimes omniscient narrators comment on characters and action using the first person. If so they are called **intrusive**. Dickens uses this technique in *A Christmas Carol*.

> ### Key Point
>
> When analysing a literary text, always consider the 'narrative voice' and your reaction to it.

> ### Key Words
>
> exposition
> inciting incident
> turning point
> climax
> protagonist
> narrator
> narrative
> omniscient narrator
> intrusive narrator

> ### Quick Test
>
> 1. Does the exposition come at the beginning or end?
> 2. When the narrator is part of the action is it a first-person or third-person narrative?
> 3. Which comes first: the climax or the inciting incident?
> 4. What is an omniscient narrator?

Creative Reading 2

You must be able to:

- Read and understand a range of literature
- Critically evaluate texts.

Character

- We learn about **characters** in different ways.
- The narrator can directly describe a character. In this example (from *The Strange Case of Dr Jekyll and Mr Hyde*) we can infer something about the man's character from his appearance.

> …the lawyer was a man of a rugged countenance, that was never lighted by a smile.

- We can learn about characters from what they say and how they say it, as well as from what other characters say about and to them. In this quotation from *Pride and Prejudice* Mr Bennet gives his opinion of his daughters:

> 'They are all silly and ignorant like other girls; but Lizzy has something more of quickness than her sisters.'

We can infer from this that Lizzy is the only daughter that Mr Bennet is interested in and that he can be quite blunt and dismissive. However, we might get a slightly different impression if we know that he is talking to his wife. It could be that he is trying to provoke her and/or that his remark about the girls being 'silly and ignorant' is intended as a joke.

- Most importantly, you should consider how characters behave and how others react to them. Dickens leaves us in no doubt about Scrooge's character:

> Even the blindmen's dogs appeared to know him; and when they saw him coming on, would tug their owners into doorways and up courts.

This comes at the beginning of *A Christmas Carol* and gives us a strong first impression, which is built on by descriptions of his treatment of his clerk, his nephew and the men who come collecting for charity.

Description

- This description (from *The Withered Arm* by Thomas Hardy) is fairly simple:

  > …it was not a main road; and the long white riband of gravel that stretched before them was empty, save for one moving speck.

  This tells us that the story is set in a remote place and sets up the encounter between the people in the carriage and the boy, whom they first see as a 'moving speck'.

- In the first chapter of *Great Expectations*, Dickens describes the setting in a way that gives us information about the landscape while creating an atmosphere that prepares us for the frightening event that is about to happen:

  > …and that the dark flat wilderness beyond the churchyard, intersected with dykes and mounds and gates, with scattered cattle feeding on it, was the marshes; and that the low leaden line beyond, was the river; and that the distant savage lair from which the wind was rushing, was the sea…

  Dickens uses adjectives like 'dark', 'low' and 'leaden' to give us a sense of an unattractive, featureless landscape, but adds words like 'wilderness' and 'savage' to make it seem dangerous and threatening.

- The description above uses literal imagery to create mood and atmosphere, the lonely, rather frightening place reflecting the feelings of the protagonist Pip.
- Figurative imagery, too, is often used in descriptive writing. In *The Withered Arm* Hardy uses a simile to describe one of his characters:

  > Her face too was fresh in colour, but it was of a totally different quality – soft and evanescent, like the light under a heap of rose-petals.

  The imagery helps us to picture her complexion and gives us a sense of her beauty and fragility.

> ### Key Point
>
> Writers describe places to root their stories in a time and place, and to create mood and atmosphere.

Quick Test

Identify what kind of imagery is being used in these sentences:
1. The lake shone like a silver mirror.
2. Angry crags surrounded us.
3. A veil of snow hid it from view.
4. There was a cluster of jagged black rocks.

> ### Key Words
>
> character
> setting
> atmosphere
> literal imagery
> mood
> figurative imagery

Reading Non-fiction 1

You must be able to:

- Read and understand a range of non-fiction texts
- Compare writers' ideas and perspectives.

Viewpoints and Perspectives

- Paper 2 of the English Language exam requires you to compare two non-fiction texts.
- The exam is called 'Writers' Viewpoints and Perspectives'. In order to understand **viewpoints** and **perspectives** you are expected to consider writers' opinions, ideas and feelings.

Form, Purpose and Audience

- Your texts could come from a number of **non-fiction forms** and **genres**. The most likely are discussed below.
- Think about the writer's purpose. It could be to describe, to inform and explain, to argue, to persuade or to advise. Remember that a text can have more than one purpose.
- Think about the intended audience. It might be aimed at people of a certain age (children, teenagers, older people). It could be intended for people in a particular job or with particular interests: for example, doctors, gardeners, cyclists. It might, however, be written for a general audience or with no audience in mind.

> **Key Point**
>
> Non-fiction is any writing that is not made up by the writer. It is not necessarily fact but it is what the writer believes to be true.

Diaries

- Diaries and **journals** are very personal. They are written by people who want to keep a record of what they have done and to express their opinions and feelings about what is happening around them.
- They can seem very immediate and spontaneous. We expect to get a genuine, uncensored and sincere point of view.
- They also give us an insight into what people really did and thought in the past.
- However, many diaries have been edited. We can still learn what the writer thought at the time of writing but it may not be exactly what he or she wrote.
- Some diaries may have been written with publication in mind by writers conscious of giving their 'version' of events.
- Diaries can vary a lot in style. Some use chatty, **informal language**. Others are quite formal.
- Some **diarists** jot down impressions and thoughts in a quite disorganized way. Other diaries are considered and crafted.

Letters

- Letters can give us an insight into people's everyday lives. Their style and tone depend a lot on their purpose.
- Letters give news and opinions, discuss ideas and express feelings. Letters might also be asking for something (like a job), complaining about something, or thanking someone for something.
- Unlike diarists, letter writers are always conscious of their audience. A letter to a close friend would be different in tone, style and content from a letter to a grandmother. It would be very different from a letter to a newspaper about current events, or to a prospective employer.
- The tone of a letter – friendly, angry, ironic, cold – will tell you a lot about the relationship between the writer and the **recipient** at the time of writing.

Autobiography and Biography

- **Biography** means writing about life. **Autobiography** means writing about one's own life.
- An autobiography can be reflective, even 'confessional', as the writer considers his or her past actions. It may also be self-justifying, naive or untrue. Autobiographies written by current celebrities (or their 'ghostwriters') are often written with the purpose of promoting the subject's career.
- Biographies range from what are known as 'hatchet jobs', designed to ruin their subjects' reputations, to 'hagiographies' (originally written about saints), which have nothing but good to say. Most are something in between.
- A biographer's point of view may come from his or her own relationship with the subject. On the other hand, it might be based on a careful consideration of the evidence.

> ### Key Point
>
> An autobiography is written by someone looking back on events, and so has the benefit of hindsight.

> ### Key Words
>
> viewpoint
> perspective
> non-fiction
> form
> genre
> journal
> informal language
> diarist
> recipient
> biography
> autobiography

> ### Quick Test
>
> Where are you most likely to find the following?
> 1. An account of someone's whole life.
> 2. Thanks for a present.
> 3. The writer's secret feelings.
> 4. How the writer became a megastar.

Reading Non-fiction 2

You must be able to:

- Read and understand a range of non-fiction texts
- Compare writers' ideas and perspectives.

Travel Writing

- Travel writing includes newspaper and magazine articles about places to visit, which give readers opinions and advice about a place. These are similar to reviews.
- You are more likely to be given autobiographical accounts of more adventurous trips – a journey down the Amazon or climbing a mountain in the Himalayas. These contain information about the places described but are more concerned with the personal experience of challenge and adventure.
- Some writers might seem awestruck and/or delighted by everything they encounter. Others are more critical, especially when writing about people and their way of life. They might even give opinions on political or other controversial issues.
- Some writers use the techniques of fiction writers to build suspense and involve readers. Others go in for colourful, even poetic description. Some write wittily about their reactions to new experiences.
- Some writers are experts, perhaps using a lot of unfamiliar terminology, for example, about mountaineering. Others see themselves as naive travellers – 'innocents abroad' – who tell jokes at their own expense.

> ### Key Point
>
> Many non-fiction texts use 'literary' techniques associated with fiction.

Journalism

- Journalism is anything that is published in a newspaper or magazine.
- Newspaper reports give the news and are mainly factual. Features – in both newspapers and magazines – look at issues in more depth. Sometimes they are balanced discussions. They can, however, strongly argue for a point of view.
- Articles can be serious or amusing. Most newspapers have regular feature writers. Some of them write about themselves and their families in a way that encourages readers to empathize with them. Others focus on more controversial issues.

- Most magazines are aimed at particular readerships – for example, women, men, teenagers, older people.
- Newspapers are aimed at a general, adult audience. However, different newspapers have different readerships, often associated with particular political views.

Reviews

- A review is an article that gives a point of view about, for example, a film, book, concert, game or restaurant.

- Reviews give information, such as venue, date, time and price. Their main purpose, however, is to give the writer's point of view.
- Some reviews are quite balanced, giving positive and negative views, though they usually do arrive at a judgement. Others express their views very strongly, sometimes in a witty way.

Comparing Points of View

- The two sources you are given will be about similar subjects but written from different points of view:
  - Compare how the writers convey different attitudes to the environment.
- You should discuss what these attitudes are:

Smith feels that we need to save rural areas, whereas Jones is happy for towns to expand.

- The attitudes shown in the sources might be directly stated or implied:

While Williams is shocked at the idea of women doing 'men's work', Roberts seems not to share the view as she does not comment on the fact that the engineer is a woman.

- Think about the impression you get of the writer:

Jones is clearly an expert on the subject, while Smith writes as a confused voter.

- Consider the general tone:

Williams uses humour to make his point, but Roberts writes seriously about her emotions.

- And remember to comment on structure and language:

Jones's use of subheadings breaks the article into clear 'points', making it more accessible.

Smith uses slang, trying to appeal to young readers, whereas Jones uses formal, quite technical language.

> **Key Point**
>
> Remember that you are being asked to compare the writers' views, not to give your own.

Quick Test

In which of the following are you least likely to find the writer's point of view?
1. A review.
2. A news report.
3. A feature.
4. Travel writing.

> **Key Words**
>
> article
> autobiographical
> journalism
> report
> feature
> review
> source

Read the passage below, which is the opening of *The Withered Arm* by Thomas Hardy, and then answer the questions.

It was an eighty-cow dairy, and the troop of milkers, regular and supernumerary, were all at work; [...] The hour was about six in the evening, and three-fourths of the large, red, rectangular animals having been finished off, there was opportunity for a little conversation.

'He do bring home his bride tomorrow, I hear. They've come as far as Anglebury today.'

The voice seemed to proceed from the belly of the cow called Cherry, but the speaker was a milking-woman, whose face was buried in the flank of that motionless beast.

'Hav' anybody seen her?' said another.

There was a negative response from the first. 'Though they say she's a rosy-cheeked, tisty-tosty little body enough,' she added; and as the milkmaid spoke she turned her face so that she could glance past her cow's tail to the other side of the barton,[1] where a thin fading woman of thirty milked somewhat apart from the rest.

'Years younger than he, they say,' continued the second, with also a glance of reflectiveness in the same direction.

'How old do you call him, then?'

'Thirty or so.'

'More like forty,' broke in an old milkman [...]

The discussion waxed so warm that the purr of the milk streams became jerky, till a voice from another cow's belly cried with authority, 'Now then, what the Turk do it matter to us about Farmer Lodge's age, or Farmer Lodge's new mis'ess? [...] Get on with your work, or 'twill be dark afore we have done. The evening is pinking in a'ready.' This speaker was the dairyman himself, by whom the milkmaids and men were employed.

Nothing more was said publicly about Farmer Lodge's wedding, but the first woman murmured under her cow to her next neighbour. ''Tis hard for she,' signifying the thin worn milkmaid aforesaid.

'O no,' said the second. 'He ha'n't spoke to Rhoda Brook for years.'

When the milking was done they washed their pails and hung them on a many-forked stand made as usual of the peeled limb of an oak-tree, set upright in the earth, and resembling a colossal antlered horn. The majority then dispersed in various directions homeward. The thin woman who had not spoken was joined by a boy of twelve or thereabout, and the twain[2] went away up the field also.

Their course lay apart from that of the others, to a lonely spot high above the water-meads, and not far from the border of Egdon Heath, whose dark countenance was visible in the distance as they drew nigh to their home.

'They've just been saying down in barton that your father brings his young wife home from Anglebury tomorrow,' the woman observed. 'I shall want to send you for a few things to market, and you'll be pretty sure to meet 'em.'

'Yes, Mother,' said the boy. 'Is Father married then?'

'Yes...You can give her a look, and tell me what she's like, if you do see her.'

[1] *barton* – cowshed
[2] *twain* – two

1 This text is the opening of a short story. How has the writer structured the text to interest you?

You could write about:
- what the writer focuses on at the beginning
- how and why the writer changes this focus as the extract develops
- any other structural features that interest you. [8]

_____

_____

_____

_____

_____

2 Halfway through this extract the writer introduces Rhoda Brook. What impression do you get of her?

In your response you could:
- write about the attitude of the other characters to her
- evaluate the ways in which the writer describes her
- support your answer with quotations from the text. [20]

_____

_____

_____

_____

_____

_____

_____

_____

_____

Source A

Source A is an article from *The Times* newspaper, 15 May 1914.

The Cult of Little Dogs: An Irresistible Appeal by Our Correspondent

There is a certain melancholy attaching to shows of toy dogs. Not that toy dogs are themselves melancholy – indeed it is their sprightly unconsciousness of their degeneracy that most confounds the moralist – but that they suggest melancholy reflections. The Englishman, perhaps alone among the peoples of the world, understands fully the great soul of the dog; he feels his own kinship with it – as he did in former days with that of the fighting cock; and he has accepted with pride the bull-dog as the type of his national qualities. It is not, then, without misgiving that he watches the process of minimizing the dog, or a large proportion of him, in an eager competition to crib, cabin, and confine the great soul in the smallest possible body, until, in place of the dignified friend and ally of man, there will be left nothing but, at worst, a pampered toy; at best, a pathetic creature, all eyes and nerves, whose insurgent soul frets the puny body to decay.

Where will the process end? Already we have held up to the admiration of the world a Pomeranian puppy which, at the age of three months, can be comfortably bestowed in a tumbler, over the edge of which his picture shows him looking, with shy eyes and apprehensively, at the disproportionate scheme of things. Presently, maybe, we shall have a childhood's dream realized and really see the little dog of the fairy-story who was hidden in a walnut and, when the shell was cracked, leapt forth barking and wagging his tail to the delight of all the noble company.

Source B

Source B is a letter to a newspaper

14 Raglan Terrace
Tillingbourne

12 July 2015

Dear Editor,

I was saddened to read yet more negative coverage of so-called 'purse pets' in your paper. What is it about celebrities who own small dogs that inspires such vitriol?

I know some people think celebrities use their pets as fashion accessories – and this is questionable. But it is not, as you suggest, cruel. We like to think of our four-legged friends as free and independent spirits – equal companions on life's journey – but they're not. Dogs depend on us for food, shelter and love.

This is the case whether they are tiny little chihuahuas that can fit in a Versace handbag or massive Afghans – or even breeds like pit bulls. Now, I don't want to be accused of the kind of prejudice I'm criticizing others for, but let's just reflect for a moment. Which is crueller? Pampering your pet with little treats or training her to fight and kill other dogs?

Of course, I'm not saying that all Staffie owners do this. But you should not imply that everyone who owns a little dog is cruel. Taking dogs shopping for little doggy clothes is a bit silly, but it does not damage their health or well-being. On the contrary, it shows that the owners care about their pets. In fact, many celebrity dog owners go further to show they care. Actress Kristin Chenoweth has even founded a charity, named after her tiny Maltese, to help homeless pets.

These dogs are beautiful, loyal and lovable. I know. I've got one. I don't keep her in my handbag or take her to canine boutiques, but I love and cherish her – and I wouldn't be without her. I don't think you'd write an article castigating me for those feelings, so why aim your vitriol at Paris Hilton and Mariah Carey, whose only crime is to love their pets?

Yours faithfully

Joanna P. Hanlon

3 Refer only to Source A. How does the writer use language to express his feelings about small dogs?

_____

_____

_____

_____

_____

_____

_____

_____ [12]

4 Refer to both Source A and Source B.

Compare how the two writers convey different attitudes to small dogs.

In your answer you should:
- compare their attitudes
- compare the methods they use to convey their attitudes
- support your ideas with quotations from both texts.

Write your answer on a separate piece of paper. [16]

Read the passage below and then answer the questions.

In this extract from *The Hound of the Baskervilles* by Sir Arthur Conan Doyle, Dr Mortimer is telling Sherlock Holmes and Dr Watson about the death of Sir Charles Baskerville, who believed his family was cursed and haunted by a mysterious beast.

'It was at my advice that Sir Charles was about to go to London. His heart was, I knew, affected, and the constant anxiety in which he lived, however chimerical[1] the cause of it might be, was evidently having a serious effect upon his health. I thought that a few months among the distractions of town would send him back a new man. Mr Stapleton, a mutual friend who was much concerned at his state of health, was of the same opinion. At the last instant came this terrible catastrophe.

'On the night of Sir Charles's death Barrymore, the butler who made the discovery, sent Perkins the groom on horseback to me, and as I was sitting up late I was able to reach Baskerville Hall within an hour of the event. I checked and corroborated all the facts which were mentioned at the inquest. I followed the footsteps down the yew alley, I saw the spot at the moor-gate where he seemed to have waited, I remarked the change in the shape of the prints after that point, I noted that there were no other footsteps save those of Barrymore on the soft gravel, and finally I carefully examined the body, which had not been touched until my arrival. Sir Charles lay on his face, his arms out, his fingers dug into the ground, and his features convulsed with some strong emotion to such an extent that I could hardly have sworn to his identity. There was certainly no physical injury of any kind. But one false statement was made by Barrymore at the inquest. He said that there were no traces upon the ground round the body. He did not observe any. But I did – some little distance off, but fresh and clear.'

'Footprints?'

'Footprints.'

'A man's or a woman's?'

Dr Mortimer looked strangely at us for an instant, and his voice sank almost to a whisper as he answered:

'Mr Holmes, they were the footprints of a gigantic hound!'

---

[1] *chimerical* – fanciful or imagined

1 This extract comes from the end of the second chapter of *The Hound of the Baskervilles*, a detective story featuring Sherlock Holmes.

How has the writer structured the text to interest you as a reader?

You could write about:
- how Dr Mortimer builds up to the discovery of the body
- how the information about the footprints is revealed
- any other structural features that interest you.

_____

_____

_____

_____

_____

_____ [8]

2 Look at the whole text.

What impression do you get of the narrator and his story?
- Write about your impressions of Dr Mortimer and his story.
- Evaluate how the writer has created these impressions.
- Support your opinions with quotations from the text.

Write your answer on a separate piece of paper. [20]

Read the passage below and answer the questions that follow.

In this extract from 'Tickets, Please', D. H. Lawrence describes the trams of an English mining area, and the people who work on them, during the First World War.

To ride on these cars is always an adventure. Since we are in war-time, the drivers are men unfit for active service: cripples and hunchbacks. So they have the spirit of the devil in them. The ride becomes a steeple-chase.[1] Hurray! We have leapt in a clear jump over the canal bridges – now for the four-lane corner. With a shriek and a trail of sparks we are clear again. To be sure, a tram often leaps the rails – but what matter! It sits in a ditch till other trams come to haul it out. It is quite common for a car, packed with one solid mass of living people, to come to a dead halt in the midst of unbroken blackness, the heart of nowhere on a dark night, and for the driver and the girl conductor[2] to call, 'All get off – car's on fire!' Instead, however, of rushing out in a panic, the passengers stolidly reply: 'Get on – get on! We're not coming out. We're stopping where we are. Push on, George.' So till flames actually appear.

The reason for this reluctance to dismount is that the nights are howlingly cold, black, and windswept, and a car is a haven of refuge. From village to village the miners travel, for a change of cinema, of girl, of pub. The trams are desperately packed. Who is going to risk himself in the black gulf outside, to wait perhaps an hour for another tram, then to see the forlorn notice 'Depot Only', because there is something wrong! Or to greet a unit of three bright cars all so tight with people that they sail past with a howl of derision. Trams that pass in the night.

This, the most dangerous tram-service in England, as the authorities themselves declare, with pride, is entirely conducted by girls, and driven by rash young men, a little crippled, or by delicate young men, who creep forward in terror. The girls are fearless young hussies.[3] In their ugly blue uniform, skirts up to their knees, shapeless old peaked caps on their heads, they have all the *sang-froid*[4] of an old non-commissioned officer. With a tram packed with howling colliers, roaring hymns downstairs and a sort of antiphony[5] of obscenities upstairs, the lasses are perfectly at their ease. They pounce on the youths who try to evade their ticket-machine. They push off the men at the end of their distance. They are not going to be done in the eye – not they. They fear nobody – and everybody fears them.

'Hello, Annie!'

'Hello, Ted!'

'Oh, mind my corn, Miss Stone. It's my belief you've got a heart of stone, for you've trod on it again.'

'You should keep it in your pocket,' replies Miss Stone, and she goes sturdily upstairs in her high boots.

'Tickets, please.'

---

[1] *steeple-chase* – a horse race over fences
[2] *conductor* – someone who sells tickets on a tram, bus or train
[3] *hussies* – cheeky or immoral girls
[4] *sang-froid* – coolness
[5] *antiphony* – singing in responses (usually in hymns)

3 According to the passage, which of the following statements are TRUE?
Tick the correct answers.

a) The trams are driven by women. ☐

b) Trams often come off the rails. ☐

c) Passengers are reluctant to leave the trams when told there's a fire. ☐

d) The girls are easily shocked. ☐

e) People are afraid of the girl conductors. ☐

f) Riding on the trams is a very boring experience. ☐

g) Not many people use the trams. ☐

h) The kind of people who work on the trams has changed because of the war. ☐ [4 marks]

4 Look in detail at the first paragraph. How does the writer use language here to describe the atmosphere on the trams?

You could include the writer's choice of:
- words and phrases
- language features and techniques
- sentence forms.

Write your answer on a separate piece of paper. [8 marks]

5 Now think about the whole text.

This extract comes near the beginning of a short story.

How has the writer structured the text to interest you as a reader?

You could write about:
- what the writer focuses on at the beginning
- how and why he changes this focus
- any other structural features that interest you.

Write your answer on a separate piece of paper. [8 marks]

6 Think about the whole text.

What impression do you get of the people who work on the trams and who use them?
- Write about your own impressions of the people.
- Evaluate how the writer has created these impressions.
- Support your opinions with quotations from the text.

Write your answer on a separate piece of paper. [20 marks]

Source A

An Extract from the Journal of Dorothy Wordsworth

Thursday 15 April 1802

It was a threatening, misty morning, but mild. We set off after dinner from Eusemere. Mrs Clarkson went a short way with us, but turned back. The wind was furious and we thought we must have returned. We first rested in the large boat-house, then under a furze bush opposite Mr Clarkson's. Saw the plough going into the field. The wind seized our breath. The lake was rough. There was a boat by itself floating in the middle of the bay below Water Millock. We rested again in the Water Millock Lane. The hawthornes are black and green, the birches here and there greenish, but there is yet more of purple to be seen on the twigs. We got over into a field to avoid some cows – people working. A few primroses by the roadside – woodsorrel flower, the anemone, scentless violets, strawberries, and that starry yellow flower which Mrs C. calls pile wort. When we were in the woods beyond Gowbarrow Park we saw a few daffodils close to the water-side. We fancied that the lake had floated the seeds ashore, and that the little colony had so sprung up. But as we went along there were more and yet more; and at last, under the boughs of the trees, we saw that there was a long belt of them along the shore, about the breadth of a country turnpike road. I never saw daffodils so beautiful. They grew among the mossy stones about and about them; some rested their heads upon those stones as on a pillow for weariness; and the rest tossed and reeled and danced, and seemed as if they verily laughed with the wind that blew upon them over the lake; they looked so gay, ever glancing, ever changing.

Source B

Blog Entry

Betsy's Blog, 2nd June

Yesterday was a complete washout. First, it was a two-hour trip in the rickety school minibus squashed in with rucksacks, suitcases and sweaty bodies.

We made it – just – and were decanted from ancient minibus into even more ancient, more rickety and smellier youth hostel. Six in a room! It's like the workhouse in Dickens. We were barely given time to unpack – although time enough to notice that Anoushka O'Reilly had brought six pairs of high-heeled shoes and eight towels – before the Camp Commandant, alias Miss Frobisher, marched in with her whistle round her neck.

'Right, girls! Gentle walk round the lake before lunch!' Gentle! It was like one of those forced marches they do in boot camps. Hours of wading through mud and getting soaked to our skins. As for the wonderful scenery we were promised. What scenery? We could barely see six inches in front of our faces through the driving rain.

Thankfully, today's been a huge improvement – they took us to an assault course thing, swinging on ropes and stuff, which is a lot better than boring walking. And there was actually a shop and a café – so I was able to replace my lost energy with a massive dose of CAKE. So now I'm feeling maybe the country's not so bad – as long as we don't have to stay much longer.

7 Refer only to Source A.

How does the writer use language to express the feelings inspired by her walk? [12]

_____

_____

_____

_____

_____

_____

_____

_____

_____

_____

_____

_____

8 Refer to both Source A and Source B.

Compare how the two writers convey different attitudes to the countryside.

In your answer you should:
- compare their attitudes
- compare the methods they use to convey their attitudes
- support your ideas with quotations from both texts.

Write your answer on a separate piece of paper. [16]

Read the sources below and answer the questions that follow.

Source A

In the extract below, taken from *Pictures from Italy*, Charles Dickens describes his visit to Florence in the 1840s.

But, how much beauty of another kind is here, when, on a fair clear morning, we look, from the summit of a hill, on Florence! See where it lies before us in a sun-lighted valley, bright with the winding Arno, and shut in by swelling hills; its domes, and towers, and palaces, rising from the rich country in a glittering heap, and shining in the sun like gold!

Magnificently stern and sombre are the streets of beautiful Florence; and the strong old piles of building make such heaps of shadow, on the ground and in the river, that there is another and a different city of rich forms and fancies, always lying at our feet. Prodigious palaces, constructed for defence, with small distrustful windows heavily barred, and walls of great thickness formed of huge masses of rough stone, frown, in their old sulky state, on every street. In the midst of the city – in the Piazza of the Grand Duke, adorned with beautiful statues and the Fountain of Neptune – rises the Palazzo Vecchio, with its enormous overhanging battlements, and the Great Tower that watches over the whole town. In its courtyard – worthy of the Castle of Otranto[1] in its ponderous gloom – is a massive staircase that the heaviest waggon and the stoutest team of horses might be driven up. Within it, is a Great Saloon, faded and tarnished in its stately decorations, and mouldering by grains, but recording yet, in pictures on its walls, the triumphs of the Medici and the wars of the old Florentine people. The prison is hard by, in an adjacent court-yard of the building – a foul and dismal place, where some men are shut up close, in small cells like ovens; and where others look through bars and beg; where some are playing draughts, and some are talking to their friends, who smoke, the while, to purify the air; and some are buying wine and fruit of women-vendors; and all are squalid, dirty, and vile to look at. 'They are merry enough, Signore,' says the jailer. 'They are all blood-stained here,' he adds, indicating, with his hand, three-fourths of the whole building. Before the hour is out, an old man, eighty years of age, quarrelling over a bargain with a young girl of seventeen, stabs her dead, in the market-place full of bright flowers; and is brought in prisoner, to swell the number.

---

[1] *Castle of Otranto* – the setting of a popular Gothic horror story of the same name

Source B

In this article for *The Times* (13 October 1982) Joyce Rackham discusses the problems caused by tourism in the Italian city of Florence.

FLORENCE: A city of dilemma

by Joyce Rackham

The bust of Benvenuto Cellini looks down sternly on the tourists littering the Ponte Vecchio. The younger ones loll – even sleep beneath him. Graffiti, although rarer than in the past, still scar some walls, and there is a very ugly souvenir stall. Yet the bridge is lined with fine shops, including jewellers whose best work follows Cellini's tradition of superb craftsmanship.

This scene reflects the dilemma of contemporary Florence – a matchless medieval city which has to stand up to the pressures, dirt and overcrowding of life in the 1980s.

Dr Silvio Abboni, a heart specialist who is also cultural assessor of the municipality, told me: 'We are victims of our big tourist boom. Florence was built as a fortress to withstand invaders. Now we must defend ourselves against too much mass tourism and potential speculators.'

Among his solutions are promoting itineraries off the beaten track, which will be published for visitors, as well as out of season attractions, both artistic and musical. He said that traffic jams could be intolerable in Florence and pointed to a new map showing plans to restrict car and bus parking and extend pedestrian precincts 'to allow city life to unfold in an orderly and pleasant manner'.

Dr Giorgio Chiarelli, Director of the Florence Tourist Board, said: 'We are a Renaissance city with about half a million inhabitants and an annual influx of around two million tourists.' He admitted that traffic pollution, litter and policing had been neglected, but said that this was changing.

Off-season tourism, with special art weekends from November to March, as well as extended shop and museum hours and more accommodation for young tourists, are intended to help ease pressures. The great Uffizi Gallery, the first public museum in the world, built by the Medici, celebrates its 400th anniversary this year. Professor Luciano Berti, its director since 1969, is also superintendent of the artistic and historic patrimony of Florence. 'Restoration is a continuous necessity and costs a great deal of money, and we don't have enough', he told me. 'We are most anxious that people see far more than the Uffizi. We cannot cope with a further growth of crowds. Since 1975 their volume has doubled.' He explained that dust from clothes and tramping feet, humidity from breath and wet clothes all have an adverse effect on paintings, many of which are now protected by glass. Crowd control measures are helping, as are the extended hours. Since August the Uffizi and most important museums, which used to close at 2pm, have been open until 7pm.

9 Read again the first five paragraphs of Source B (from 'The bust' to 'changing').

According to the article, which four of the following statements are TRUE?

- Shade the boxes of the ones you think are true.
- Choose a maximum of four statements.

a) The souvenir stall at the Ponte Vecchio is very attractive. ☐

b) There are shops on the bridge. ☐

c) There is no pollution in Florence. ☐

d) Dr Abboni believes the increase in tourists has been bad for Florence. ☐

e) Florence is a modern city. ☐

f) The jewellers produce some very good work. ☐

g) The authorities in Florence are encouraging tourists to go to less well-known parts of the city. ☐

h) Dr Abboni wants to ban tourists from Florence. ☐ [4 marks]

10 You need to refer to Source A and Source B for this question.

Use details from both sources.

Write a summary of the differences between the two descriptions of Florence. [8 marks]

11 You need only to refer to Source A for this question.

How does Dickens use language to convey his impressions of Florence? [12 marks]

12 For this question you need to refer to the whole of Source A together with the whole of Source B.

Compare how the two writers convey their different reactions to the city of Florence.

In your answer you should:
- compare their different reactions
- compare the methods they use to convey their reactions
- support your ideas with quotations from both texts. [16 marks]

Answers

Page 5 Quick Test
1. Openly stated. **2.** Yes. **3.** Yes. **4.** No.
Page 7 Quick Test
1. The writer. **2.** The reader. **3.** No.
4. You get no marks.
Page 9 Quick Test
1. Yes. **2.** Yes. **3.** No. **4.** No.

Page 11 Quick Test
1. Quotation and paraphrase.
2. Everything that is in the original text.
3. When it does not fit easily into the sentence.
4. Point, Evidence, Explanation (or Exploration).

Page 13 Quick Test
1. Horse and oats. **2.** Was munching.
3. Old. **4.** On. **5.** Thoughtfully.
Page 15 Quick Test
1. Personification. **2.** Alliteration.
3. Simile. **4.** Metaphor.
Page 17 Quick Test
1. b, c, d, a **2.** a, d, c, b **3.** c, a, b, d

1. • Nobody greeted him cheerfully.
   • People did not ask him to come and see them.
   • Beggars did not beg from him.
   • Children did not ask him for the time.
   • Nobody asked him the way anywhere.
   [Maximum 4 marks]

2.

Marks	Skills	Examples of possible content
7–8	• You have analysed the effects of the choice of language. • You have used an appropriate range of quotations. • You have used sophisticated subject terminology appropriately.	The first complex sentence seems quite light-hearted, the direct speech reflecting a polite greeting, such as people might make in the street, but the sentence starts with 'Nobody', so we know Scrooge is not like others. The next sentence builds a list of those who avoid Scrooge, starting each clause with 'no' before giving an innocuous phrase such as 'what it was o'clock'. The last sentence gives us a sense of evil, 'even the blindmen's dogs' implying that a dislike of Scrooge is natural and instinctive.
5–6	• You have clearly explained the effects of the choice of language. • You have used a range of relevant quotations. • You have used subject terminology appropriately.	In three sentences, each one longer than the last, the writer gives lists of different sorts of people, starting phrases with the repeated 'no', to give a general negative impression. When he imagines what the dogs might say he uses the adjectives 'dark' and 'evil' to show that Scrooge is feared.

   [Maximum 8 marks]
3. b, c, e, f   **[Maximum 4 marks]**
4.

Marks	Skills	Examples of possible content
7–8	• You have given a perceptive interpretation of both texts. • You have synthesized evidence from texts. • You have used appropriate quotations from both texts.	Although the writers have opposite views – Weston is a 'city-hater' but Lamb never wants to 'see a mountain in my life' – they are both careful not to insult people who have the opposite view ('I could gang anywhere'; 'Sorry, Londoners'). Lamb lists things like 'crowded streets' that he likes. These are the things Weston hates, calling it 'dirty' and 'noisy'. Weston knows 'it's meant to be…exciting' and this is clearly Lamb's view.
5–6	• You have started to interpret both texts. • You have shown clear connections between texts. • You have used relevant quotations from both texts.	Lamb explains that he has always lived in London so cannot see the attraction of the countryside. Weston, on the other hand, calls the country 'home' and thinks this is why he is bored with the city. Lamb loves the shops, the theatre and even the 'wickedness', but Weston can only see how 'expensive' it is and how everyone is 'bad-tempered'.

   [Maximum 8 marks]
5. a, c, d, f   **[Maximum 4 marks]**
6. See 'Skills' column of table above (for Q4).

Marks	Examples of possible content
7–8	It took Brontë a long time to get published. She had to work out the 'puzzle' of why no-one was interested and look for advice. Fordyce, on the other hand, was published quickly and is often asked for advice by other poets. They also had very different experiences of being a woman poet. Brontë had a 'vague impression' that her sex would be a disadvantage, but Fordyce, who was 'welcomed with enthusiasm' by other poets, feels it was a positive thing for her.
5–6	The Brontës thought they might be 'looked on with prejudice' because they were women, whereas Fordyce thinks her gender was an advantage ('we don't get enough women'). Fordyce wrote to magazines and performed her poetry live, but for Brontë the only way was to write to publishers, who did not reply.

[Maximum 8 marks]

7.

Marks	Skills	Examples of possible content
10–12	• You have analysed the effects of the choice of language. • You have used an appropriate range of quotations. • You have used sophisticated subject terminology appropriately.	Fordyce gives advice in a clear, colloquial tone, as if she is talking to a friend: 'All I can do is say'. She is also modest, using the noun 'luck' three times and the adjective 'lucky' once, though this is balanced by the repetition of references to 'hard work'. She uses short, often simple sentences – 'It wasn't that hard for me' – which helps make the process seem simple. Using the metaphor 'magic key' in the first paragraph could make readers think she is saying she can't help, but this impression is contradicted by the rest of the passage, as she does try to help.
7–9	• You have clearly explained the effects of the choice of language. • You have used a range of relevant quotations. • You have used subject terminology appropriately.	Fordyce writes in a chatty, straightforward way, getting straight to the point with 'People often ask me'. She uses a metaphor, 'magic key', to show that there is no easy answer, but her tone is helpful. She emphasizes that this is her personal experience by constant use of the first person.

[Maximum 12 marks]

Pages 22–29 Revise Questions

Page 23 Quick Test
1. The beginning. 2. First.
3. The inciting incident.
4. One who knows everything.

Page 25 Quick Test
1. Simile.
2. Personification/pathetic fallacy.
3. Metaphor. 4. Literal imagery.

Page 27 Quick Test
1. Biography. 2. Letter.
3. Diary. 4. Autobiography.
Page 29 Quick Test
2 (news report).

Pages 30–33 Practice Questions

1.

Marks	Skills	Examples of possible content
7–8	• You have analysed the use of structural features. • You have chosen an appropriate range of examples. • You have used a range of subject terminology accurately.	The text is written to gradually reveal to the reader who the 'thin woman' is and what her situation is. It starts by setting the scene in the 'barton', giving us an idea of the kind of people the story is about, just mentioning Rhoda briefly. The direct speech of the milkers tells us (and Rhoda) about the farmer's bride. When the dairyman tells them to stop, two brief lines of dialogue bring Rhoda into focus as having an interest in the farmer. At the end the focus shifts to Rhoda and her son. Through their dialogue, the writer reveals why she has an interest in the farmer, and the last thing she says leaves us wondering why she is so keen to hear about the bride and what might be the result of her curiosity.
5–6	• You have clearly explained the effect of structural features. • You have chosen relevant examples. • You have used subject terminology accurately.	At the beginning the focus is on the milking shed and we get an idea of their daily lives. The writer uses direct speech to tell us about the farmer getting married, and the last bit of dialogue tells us it has something to do with the 'worn milkmaid'. Then the focus changes to the worn milkmaid as she meets her son after work. Their conversation reveals to us that the farmer is the boy's father.

[Maximum 8 marks]

2.

Marks	Skills	Examples of possible content
16–20	• You have critically evaluated the text in a detailed way. • You have used examples from the text to explain your views convincingly. • You have analysed a range of the writer's methods. • You have used a range of relevant quotations to support your views.	Rhoda Brook is introduced as a 'thin fading woman'. She is a milkmaid, indicating her rural working-class background, but the writer's use of the phrase 'apart from the rest' suggests that she is somehow different. Perhaps she thinks she is better than the others or perhaps they look down on her. It may be a mixture of both, as the conversation between the milkers hints that she had a relationship with the farmer. The writer tells us she also lives 'apart' from others, emphasizing her solitary nature. The personification of the heath's 'dark countenance' suggests sadness and maybe mystery. This is reflected in Rhoda's nature and situation.
11–15	• You have clearly evaluated the text. • You have used examples from the text to explain your views clearly. • You have clearly explained the effect of the writer's methods. • You have used some relevant quotations to support your views.	The writer makes us interested in Rhoda Brook by not explaining anything about her but giving us hints. She is first described as 'a thin fading woman of thirty' and she does not work with the others. Perhaps she does not get on with the others or she just prefers to be alone. Because the others look at her when talking about the farmer, we can infer that she had a relationship with him. Later we find out that she had a son by him. This is scandalous and might explain why she is 'apart'.

[Maximum 20 marks]

3. Look at the mark scheme below, decide which description is closest to your answer and then decide which mark to give yourself. See 'Skills' column of table above (Practice Question Q3).

Marks	Examples of possible content
10–12	The writer's tone is quite serious and authoritative. The expression 'confounds the moralist' suggests that he is dealing with a moral problem. He uses hyperbole to show he loves dogs ('the great soul'). Other rhetorical devices he uses include the rhetorical question ('Where will the process end?') and the list of three, combined with alliteration ('crib, cabin, and confine'). He uses emotive language to make us feel sorry for the small dogs: 'frets the puny body to decay'.
7–9	The writer uses Standard English and sounds as if he knows what he's talking about. He uses impressive phrases like the 'great soul' to show he loves dogs and feels sad that they are made into 'puny' animals. He uses a rhetorical question ('Where will the process end?') to make us think about the consequences of breeding these dogs.

[Maximum 12 marks]

4. Look at the mark scheme below, decide which description is closest to your answer and then decide which mark to give yourself.

Marks	Skills	Examples of possible content
13–16	• You have compared ideas and perspectives in a perceptive way. • You have analysed methods used to convey ideas and perspectives. • You have used a range of appropriate quotations.	Both these writers are very passionate about their subject. The first writer attacks those who breed small dogs by making the dogs sound like victims ('all eyes and nerves') but also calls them 'pampered'. Hanlon picks up on this but cannot see what's wrong with pampering – she sees it as love. Her tone is chatty and personal, while his is impersonal and authoritative.
9–12	• You have compared ideas and perspectives in a clear and relevant way. • You have explained clearly methods used to convey ideas and perspectives. • You have used relevant quotations from both texts.	The writer in *The Times* uses rhetorical devices to convince his readers. He claims to love dogs but is against breeding small dogs and treating them like toys. Hanlon defends people who have small dogs, saying those who attack them are just having a go at celebrities. She too uses rhetorical questions.

[Maximum 16 marks]

Pages 34–42 **Review Questions**

1. See 'Skills' column of table on p. 43 (for p. 18–21 Practice Questions, Q2).

Marks	Examples of possible content
7–8	The writer wants to create an air of mystery and to keep the reader curious. He distances the death of Sir Charles by describing it in Dr Mortimer's speech. In his first paragraph he talks about Sir Charles's health, which the reader might think explains his death, but he ends with the word 'catastrophe'. This makes us want to know what the awful thing was. The next paragraph is about his experience on the night of the death and builds up to his revelation that there was more to it than was revealed at the inquest. This adds to the mystery but he still does not reveal his information. Holmes asks him questions that might be in the reader's mind, while delaying the shock revelation.
5–6	The doctor builds up to a revelation by describing following Sir Charles's footprints. At the end he mentions that he knows something no-one else has noticed but keeps back the information until Holmes questions him. This makes the fact that 'they were the footprints of a gigantic hound' have more impact on the reader.

[Maximum 8 marks]

2. See 'Skills' column of table on p. 44 (for p. 30–33 Practice Questions, Q2).

Marks	Examples of possible content
16–20	We are not told anything about the doctor's character, but the fact that he is a professional, scientific man implies he is a reliable witness. This is confirmed by his suspicion that Sir Charles's illness was 'chimerical', suggesting he is not easily convinced of things. He describes how he 'checked and corroborated' the evidence from the inquest, implying that he is both thorough and independent-minded. The fact that he has done this, and the careful and detailed description he gives, make the reader more inclined to accept his story than if it had been told in a sensational way.
11–15	The story of finding the footprints is far-fetched but the use of Dr Mortimer to tell it makes it more believable. This is because he is a doctor and he tells the story in a calm way, remembering details: 'I noted that there were no other footsteps save those of Barrymore on the soft gravel.' When the writer says 'his voice sank almost to a whisper', the reader gets the impression that he is scared and shocked.

[Maximum 20 marks]

3. b, c , e, h **[4]**

4. See 'Skills' column of table on p. 44 (for p. 18–21 Practice Questions, Q7).

Marks	Examples of possible content
7–8	The writer writes at first as if he is explaining something to us, describing in detail something that is happening now. The phrase 'the spirit of the devil' makes us think of evil, and the descriptions of darkness and flames might also have connotations of hell and damnation. Yet there is a sense of excitement in the extended metaphor of the horse race. The paragraph ends with a comic contrast between the danger of the fire and the passengers' down-to-earth colloquial reaction: 'We're stopping where we are. Push on, George.'
5–6	He writes in the present tense and we can imagine ourselves there. The metaphor of the 'steeple-chase' makes the tram seem like a living thing and the experience like being on a horse. There is a contrast between the 'blackness' and 'heart of nowhere', which sound ominous, and the cheerful speech of the people.

[Maximum 8 marks]

5. See 'Skills' column of table on p. 44 (for p. 30–33 Practice Questions, Q1).

Marks	Examples of possible content
7–8	The writer moves from the general to the particular. The first three paragraphs move from describing the trams as something exotic and fantastical to telling us about particular people on them. The mood changes at the start of paragraph 2 with 'the reason for this', which leads into an account of what the trams are actually used for, contrasting with the fantastical imagery of the first paragraph…
5–6	At first the focus is on the tram ride and how exciting it is, at the same time telling us about the setting. The focus shifts to the passengers and how they feel about the tram service – more of the reality of it. In the third paragraph he gives a general description of drivers and conductors. Then we have some dialogue, which brings the focus to one conductor, Annie.

[Maximum 8 marks]

6. See 'Skills' column of table on p. 44 (for pages 30–33 Practice Questions, Q2).

Marks	Examples of possible content
16–20	The writer only describes the men briefly, his main focus being the girl conductors. However, he gives a very vivid impression of the men in a few words. Although they are 'cripples and hunchbacks', who might be looked down on, especially because they are not at war, they have the 'spirit of the devil', a comparison which makes them seem exotic and exciting. The girls are introduced to us as 'fearless young hussies', implying that they do not behave in the way expected of women at the time. He goes on to compare them to non-commissioned officers. Coupled with a description of their unflattering uniform, this may not sound complimentary, but the tone of the description suggests admiration and respect…
11–15	At first the people who work on the trams sound like misfits and are described in a quite insulting way – 'cripples and hunchbacks', but then the writer says they have 'the spirit of the devil in them'. This could mean they are wicked but, from what he then says, I think he means they are reckless and brave. The girls are different because they would not be at war anyway. They are young and very confident. He calls them 'fearless young hussies', which makes them sound attractive but a bit frightening.

[Maximum 20 marks]

7. Look at the mark scheme below, decide which description is closest to your answer and then decide which mark to give yourself.
See 'Skills' column of table on p. 44 (for pages 18–21 Practice Questions, Q7).

Marks	Examples of possible content
10–12	Most of the passage is a quite straightforward account of the walk, which is what you would expect from a diary entry – it is written in the first person and the past tense and just describes what she saw, often using simple sentences ('The lake was rough'), and fragments ('A few primroses by the roadside'). The effect of this is to make it seem fresh and immediate. When she describes the daffodils she uses more 'literary' language, personifying them: they 'rested their heads' and 'reeled and danced'.
7–9	She does not always used complete sentences ('Saw the plough…') which makes it seem like she's writing notes for herself. She describes nature in great detail – 'The hawthornes are black and green' – so you can picture it. The simple sentence 'I never saw daffodils so beautiful' emphasizes her strong emotion.

[Maximum 12 marks]

8. See 'Skills' column of table on p. 45 (for pages 30–33 Practice Questions, Q4).

Marks	Examples of possible content
13–16	Wordsworth seems to be writing for herself, reflecting on her day, whereas Betsy is very aware of her audience. She uses hyperbole, 'complete washout' and 'like the workhouse', for comic effect. She writes in a colloquial way, as she might talk to her friends – 'ropes and stuff'. She also describes other members of the party in a critical yet amusing way (the Camp Commandant…with her whistle round her neck'), while Wordsworth makes no comment about her companions.
9–12	While Wordsworth clearly gets a lot of pleasure from observing nature, Betsy hates walking round the lake. Betsy is quite sarcastic and exaggerates everything for humour – 'It's like the workhouse'. Wordsworth's writing is serious and descriptive, not saying much about her feelings, but Betsy only thinks about herself.

[Maximum 16 marks]

9. b, d, f, g **[4]**

10. See 'Skills' column of table on p. 43 (for p. 18–21 Practice Questions, Q4).

Marks	Examples of possible content
7–8	Both writers say the city is beautiful. Dickens describes the view from outside the city and then the centre. Rackham describes tourist places, like the Ponte Vecchio, but says tourists are 'littering' it and also mentions graffiti and 'a very ugly souvenir stall'. Dickens does not say anything about other tourists. While Rackham focuses on the 'dilemma' facing the city, Dickens is most interested in the prison and the life of the 'blood-stained' inmates.
5–6	Dickens is very impressed by the 'magnificent' city and describes its beauty. Rackham also describes some of the attractions but talks about graffiti and an 'ugly' stall. Dickens sees a negative side of the city but for him it is the prison, next to the great castle, and the violence of a place where 'they are all blood-stained'. According to Rackham, the downside of Florence is all the tourists, who are spoiling what they come to see.

[Maximum 8 marks]

11. See 'Skills' column of table on p. 44 (for p. 18–21 Practice Questions, Q7).

Marks	Examples of possible content
10–12	In the first paragraph, Dickens uses images of light and richness to describe Florence: 'bright…glittering…like gold!' His exclamations and his use of the second person ('we') make us feel his wonder as if we were there with him. In the second paragraph, he moves into the city and his language reflects both the atmosphere and the architecture. He personifies the buildings, describing 'distrustful windows' and saying they 'frown, in their old sulky state'…
7–9	Dickens writes in the present tense and the first person ('we') as if he is telling us what happens as it happens. He describes the buildings as if they were people, saying they 'frown'. He contrasts the beautiful palaces with the prison, summing up how uncomfortable it is in the simile 'cells like ovens'.

[Maximum 12 marks]

12. See 'Skills' column of table on p. 45 (for pages 30–33 Practice Questions, Q4).

Marks	Examples of possible content
13–16	Dickens is writing about his personal experience of visiting Florence and the effect it had on him, whereas the purpose of Rackham's article is to examine the 'dilemma' of a city dependent on tourists being ruined by 'mass tourism and potential speculators'. Dickens uses hyperbolic, poetic images to describe the city 'shining in the sun like gold' but also 'stern and sombre'. Rackham starts almost by imitating Dickens as she describes a statue looking 'sternly', but for her this implies a judgement on the tourists, and from then on her focus is not on describing the city but on the issues.
9–12	Rackham writes about the issues of tourism and pollution and their effect on the city. Dickens does not mention this, perhaps because it was not a problem in his day. He describes the 'magnificent' city in detail, whereas she just sketches in a few details about the shops on the Ponte Vecchio in order to show us the 'dilemma of contemporary Florence'.

[Maximum 16 marks]

Notes